OVERTLY REVEALING
M'eye Views

Daniel Rodriguez

authorHOUSE®

AuthorHouse™
1663 Liberty Drive
Bloomington, IN 47403
www.authorhouse.com
Phone: 1 (800) 839-8640

Published by AuthorHouse 01/23/2017

ISBN: 978-1-5246-6018-5 (sc)
ISBN: 978-1-5246-6017-8 (e)

Contents

Acknowledgement

The Rodriguez name has traveled from its origin, through the evolutionary changes of the Eras and the obstacles that have become building blocks, to its continued desire of higher achievement. As governed by society, the offspring are given the family name of the father. Rodriguez was my mother's maiden name as well, so my siblings and I were blessed to carry on the family names of both our parents. Papi, was one of seven children and the five boys were musically inclined. Papi, had an incredible voice and the ability to write his own material that would one day get recorded on a 45-rpm record. Mami, was one of twelve girls so we were overwhelmed with motherly love. To be one of twelve women with only a fourth-grade education, Mami's resilience provided a blueprint on how to keep Faith and reach deep into our fortitude to overcome adversity.

The ability to converse in the choice of two native languages created the capability to gather phrases in sarcasm, humor and love which were being archived for use in the latter part of my life. During the enhancement of my career, I was challenged by term paper assignments that would trigger the recall of experiences in my life and the aspirations of expression by means of the written word.

These Episodes are dedicated to Maria Antonia (Rodriguez) Jones, (December 24th, 1932 - July 7th, 2016). Titi, as the last of the twelve you provided the family with a love and kindness that will be difficult to match. I will do my best to carry the torch as the last of my generation. You will be missed!

Volume two

Victimization that is dramatized to gain social empathy is rooted by a seed planted during a traumatic childhood episode. Witnessing such a sensationalized performance may actually cause a need to mimic depending on the ovation that it received. Cautiously regulate the verbal or physical responses as they are more likely to be sponged by the innocent offspring.

Organize any issues at hand in an order of precedence which puts all things at the same level. Picking and choosing what is easier for you will cause a glitch in the system. Though the certificate states "engineering" as a forte, common sense should always prevail. In order to keep it simple, sift through the first layers before a crater is created.

Leave an impression on those who have extended their humble abode, as billets for the duration, by actually treating the facilities above and beyond the manner in which is expected for your own dwelling. Gratitude is valued by the way it is shown, not by eloquent words that carry no weight. An offer to return with an open date is proof that behavior during the visit was superb.

Untactfully stating one sentence does not invalidate the paragraph. Emotional response to the one percent only reflects the intellectual level of the argument and exposes the talent to avoid a truthful confrontation. A luxurious wish list that diminishes the blood, sweat and tears of the laborer expresses egocentrism on behalf of the author.

Many years of being the consoler, the educator, the disciplinarian, the source of income, and the pillar of Love, has been an investment with bountiful returns. A family that continues to spread the roots of our ancestors has aspirations of becoming part of the Almighty's flock. Thank you, Heavenly Father, for the nurturing you provide.

Efforts to manage two lifestyles will ultimately lose its density like a rock being eroded by the pounding of the waves. An unbalanced outcome will tip the scale due to the weight of stress. Sometimes a gentle nudge will persuade a lazy occupant to take flight.

Take a deep breath and gently exhale, as the heart rate slows down allow the mind to pick up the surrounding events. The beauty that was created for the marvel of man has been subdued and stained by the residue of evil. The waterways have been polluted along with the development of the mind by the carelessness and the lack of passing on the significance of the purity of creation.

When the angle of demise is slightly altered, the target becomes a challenge to hit. The more negative the ammunition the larger the margin of error. The words used to belittle competence will soon describe the reflection of the wicked behavior.

Opinions, when verbalized, must be done so in an eloquent format as to not offend. We must be careful that it is not a voiced judgment as the One who would be offended is of much more importance. When a mule is used, it is a form of message transportation that surpasses the cream of the crop in the auto industry. Do not let the diamond ring's glare obscure the direction of the words.

Episode I

Love

Uncovered Deceit

Contrary to popular belief, a Father's love for his child runs just as deep as that of a mutha's. The void of their presence can only be filled by the warmth of their hug. The truth will always prevail, no matter what dirt attempts to cover it. Those that hold the shovel will wear the dirt! Justice will come with a smile!!!

Leap of Love

A tree may bare many fruits. Time is what controls the ripeness but sometimes it is best to jump for the apple before it falls for you. Trust in your heart and avoid the unfounded rules of society.

Going Up

The repetition of a sound that bounces and echoes off the outer walls only defines the emptiness found in a lonely heart. A solid thud provides evidence reaching bottom. Use love as a filler and the dents along with the cracks will be repaired.

Coffee, Tea or . . .

Positions are now available for the Mile-High Club. Applicants must be proficient in the handling of projectiles. Candidates will be required to be ambidextrous, to perform tasks from both sides of the spectrum. To qualify, nominees are required to perform in-flight missile repair.

Glutton for Punishment

Though it is written that opposites attract, pinpointing which attribute is referred to, is still a mystery. After many years of research, the "jerk" is preferred, yet the bear is much more approachable with a jar of honey. The Choice is clear but that is not what is in question.

Unhealthy Suspicion

Negative thoughts of the significant other lead to false accusations. Jealousy is a disease that eats away the mind and the true meaning of love. Trust, appreciate, and love or in the blink of an eye, the other will no longer be significant.

Fireworks

The thrill of exploring the unknown, causes adrenaline to flow so rapidly the heart can barely control its pulse. At first site attraction, will be evident and the formula for chemistry will begin. Caution as the elements mix, an explosion may be inevitable.

Safe not Sorry

It may seem heartless to part with one who loves you, but it is only just that they receive the same in return. Intense grief is experienced during the termination of a relationship that was heartfelt, no matter how gentle the conclusion. Do not extend the inevitable as misery will follow.

Technological Peephole

Research to analyze the reaction of people on the internet turned into an unbelievable time to face reality with hopes of destiny. The latch resides on your side of the gate. The access control list lies in your hands.

Photo Shop Expert

Attractive cover and catchy title will ignite the desire to open and inspect the table of contents. The intro or acknowledgement will tempt the curiosity. When the photo has been altered, it is time for an alternate ending.

Insatiable Recipe

Chemistry tutoring will not provide the formula for happiness. The ingredients are natural and vigorously rubbed on the product to produce the flavor of ecstasy. Exhilaration is the phenomenon manufactured by mutual love.

Splitting Headache

Do not blame yourself for the actions between two adults. The journey now has two paths due to the change of heart. What has been created between the two will never be divided. Only time will reveal the explanation and I pray that it will not repeat itself in you.

Catin

Unaccompanied in the latter part of your life can cause the heart to triple in size. As depression sets in, the heart inflates with sad memories and thoughts of being forgotten. I love you, thank you and will never forget you!

Painful Exodus

"Your Daddy's dead", these words have haunted the hearts of so many. The method of departure has no significance. Snatching away a unique love can never be explained. Be grateful of the present time and treasure the memories left behind.

Cracking Me Up

A moment of bonding with one parent can be an expensive laugh. Accidental annihilation of the coffee table causes evil to invade the peaceful moment. Her constant nagging did not break the glass but caused the snap of the relaxing monster.

Lower the Volume

Broom handles were thick as little league bats and made a distinctive sound when introduced to the coconut. Thought twice when the feisty woman who birthed you approached with anger. One full swing is a painful way to learn humbleness.

Walgreens Winner

No trailer was needed for the Snow Boat; just make room in the trunk. Read the fine print, as cushions and protective gear are not included. Roosevelt Park Suicide Hill should be approached with extreme caution as the signs have been stolen for amusement purposes.

All Hallows' Evening

How ironic to dress like hobos, when only one poverty level above them. There was such a joy to coordinate the outfits and smear the eyeliner pencil for the makeshift scrubby beard. Candy happiness, by any means necessary.

For Me

Wave your hands in the air and jump up and down. A priceless glance at the cell only confirmed that fool was not an attribute she possessed. The perfect smile and warm greeting topped with a stuffed animal, balloons, and flowers provided the evidence of a kindred spirit. The first night of the rest of our lives! You are my Blessing!

For the Haters

Respect the bond that unites the happy pair. Search for the element that provides the magnetism between the two and apply. Take shame in ill desires for what has not been bestowed upon you.

Mami

Half a can of Campbell's chicken noodle soup that sits on a shelf of a bare refrigerator is what was saved to complete a two-meal day. I can still feel the ripping through my heart as I dressed the never healing wound. There is so much more I could have done to show you my gratitude. May GOD be with you.

Charismatic Augmentation

Redirecting half the energy used to depict the negative in others will enhance the development of a good character. Extending a helping hand opens the path of compassion to the witnesses of the act. Carefully view the unfortunate; it may be a vision through a window of the past, or of the future.

A Plate of Empathy

How can I eat in the face of the unfortunate? When the feeling of compassion possesses the inner core, react with the spirit of giving and receive the blessing attached to look in the eye of the recipient. Follow up with a reminder of who loves us all.

Friendship Void

True friends have a way of bringing joy to the heart by way of the ear. A small message of your presence being missed will fill the void produced by the separation of time. The vision of their smile crosses my mind during my prayer of their well-being. May GOD always be with you all!

Legacy

Being a part of an unforgettable memory will last longer in only half of the parties involved. There is no greater gift than to make the survivors smile at the thought of you. Say "I love you" as many times as the thought crosses your mind so the recording will be fresh in the mind of recipient.

The Unanticipated

Window shopping with the vision of my Queen modeling the stunning apparel instills a certain desire to make it reality. The joy comes from a smile of an unexpected gift being presented at just the right time. Celebrate an anniversary each day that the Lord has blessed you to share together.

Priceless

The scenery was breath taking, the cuisine was succulent, the tropical drinks disguised the proof of liquor, and the look in her eye was one of peaceful satisfaction. Our imaginations took us to the island of the Caribbean, dressed in linen with sun hats to match. Thank you for being a part of the virgin voyage of many unforgettable weekends.

Fourth Blessing

As the focus is adjusted the surroundings become clearer. One eye opens to see the proud donor with tears of joy forming. Welcome to the first day of your life, is the thought that appears right after "Lord, thank you for making me a worthy and humble servant.

Inner Beauty

Only blessed with a beautiful heart, the rather unattractive mother found that her calling was to ensure that the mouths of her responsibility were properly fed. As the aging process took its toll, her confidence in the Lord grew. May He grant her the Prince Charming, she has faithfully anticipated.

Restoration

When tender loving care is applied to anything it will prolong its life. As the grey film is removed, what was old beauty has become new. Refurbish the used to invest in what is truly needed.

A Mother's Journey

The journey was long and prosperous leaving behind a legacy of kindness and love. Educating the lost souls in her path with the word of GOD was the mission assigned to her. Tears, no doubt will be shed for both, her absence and for her joy as her wings spread in preparation for her ascension. Thank you for your expression of the definition of love.

Sorrow Conquered

The void that is felt when a loved one is lost can be extremely challenging to fill. Treasure the memories and they will be present for an eternity. He hears your pain as a request for love but your acceptance is required for it to be granted.

Insatiability

The expectation of happiness for the one you love may be an unachievable quest when satisfaction is accepted in smaller packages. Careful the choice does not have a monetary value mindset as there may be a rude awakening to the outcome of your riches. Trust in Him for all things.

A Christmas Meal

Joy and satisfaction exposed by facial expressions during a feast fit for royalty cannot be restrained. The look in his eyes as he focused on the love of his life brought tears to all onlookers. Do not let the moments to be cherished escape as the rewind button may incur a malfunction.

Individual Interests

The importance of the event lies in the emotional attachment of the attendee. Though the significance of the invited may carry a high level of expectation the change in plans should not affect the flexibility of the relationship. A life together at times means that separation may be required without weakening the bond.

Chastisement of the Unselfish

Excitement is ruined by the drain cover hole that reaches out to grab the wheel. Unselfishly offering your body to save her will forever be a debt she will carry. Being punished for not completing the mission should not have been the reward. From both of our hearts, thanks MO!

Line in the Sand

The fog has been thick enough to cut with a machete, as levels of testosterone collide. One as the protector flexes the bond since childhood and the other with a prowess of a lion on the hunt as the meaning of Love comes to a cross road. There will always be a home field advantage for both parties involved so there will be no need to bear arms.

Liability Insurance

Concerns of how someone feels are a natural response when love is involved. No matter how something was interpreted the reaction is to want to take some or all of the blame. Know that there will have to be a cool down phase before emotional opinions are under control and that humbleness must be an attached document.

Two Lane Highways

The road of confidence is a curvy obstacle course that can be dangerous if the acceleration is not managed correctly. Revert to the unpaved path that has brought you to your current level of expertise and do not to forget the sacrifices that were invested. There is always a supporting cast so be careful when addressing achievements with "I".

Endless Guardian

As a windup toy hits the uneven surface it tumbles to the ground, the reaction is to pick it up, twist the winder and place it back on its feet. A child's memory is not of how many times they fell but of who was there to brush the dirt off their knees. No matter the age that is reached a parent's encouraging word is always heartfelt.

One Tree

One should always be grateful for the reunion of siblings that have been separated by miles of terrain and time. Though our minds travel in their own unique paths, our hearts have been carved from the blessings bestowed upon our parents. LORD, we owe you for the incredible nurturing they gave us, our creativity and loving souls.

Squandered Period

The desire to engage in a long-lasting relationship comes from the heart. Once in, give it all without inhibiting any feelings, the results will demonstrate how much time has been wasted. The focus must be on the reflection if there is any hope of being an asset to anyone else.

Revelation

Upon the initial lifting of the heavy lids the first reaction is to let them fall back to the closed position but instead the desire is to focus. The vision of an angel slowly appears during the adjustment and clarity phase. A smile quickly joins in on the sequence with the affirmation that blessings are granted by Grace.

Unprecedented Security

The moat bridge has been lowered and the castle doors opened but the issue of your horse facing the wrong direction still exists. The King's arrogance is not a hereditary attribute yet his sandals have graced the soil of the new Queen. Princess to be must release the grasp of unwarranted bondage.

Daniel Rodriguez

Artificial Emotion

As technology is invading the minds of our youth, communication levels have plummeted and the expressions between two people are now being accomplished in a text language. Courage is now being developed through the absence of the face to face. It is important to emphasize that love should occupy the majority of the hard drive.

A Bonded Commitment

Adolescence memories not only bring tears of joy or laughter tears but also the uniqueness in how the accounts were stored in our memories. Moments between pictures inspire the philosopher's wit to point out the inadequacies of what were self-appointed strengths. Family expresses what it is to accept each other for what one has become and to give a helping hand when a derailment occurs.

Episode II

Angelic

Self-pity

Though life may bring you cloudy days, it is only to prepare you for the sunshine that lies beyond. FAITH will gently wipe the tears away and relieve eye irritation caused by pity. My GOD is a good GOD and He is GOD all by Himself.

Tear Drops

The stench engages the opening of the tear ducts. A request for change to nourish the pain of hunger or alcoholism is voiced by a less fortunate. After a brisk "NO", realization of a childhood high school idol is focused and the tears are now of sorrow. Be thankful for the blessings you possess today, foolishly taking them for granted may cause tomorrow to take them away.

Strong Construction

As the waves continue to grow, so does the turmoil within the current. Though the exterior is bruised and battered, a well-constructed Faith can withstand any tsunami no matter its intensity. Believing reinforces the pillars of one's foundation and enhances security in spiritual growth.

Soul Enrichment

Like an asteroid shower, doubts attack the mind. The strongest glue that can be used to reinforce the outer walls is Faith. The belief in existence of the Creator is the belief in the invisible. Faith in the invisible nourishes the physical path of righteousness and is the fertilizer for the soul.

Situation Report

Drastic predicaments impact the rebirth of a soul. An alternative perspective on human existence will evolve with vigilance. The sit-rep is written in pencil for updating purposes and can be altered without warning.

Reassurance

The cement base of the fire escape was considered sacred ground for the juvenile. As the horizontal body stared into the clear night sky, GOD would move the stars like pieces in a chess match and acknowledge his existence. His presence was reassured and tears formed while in prayer. Thank you, Father!

Bottoms up

Testosterone levels collide when the first born becomes aware of his strength. The constant bumps to the head rearrange the priorities of what career field would be followed. The huge heart is clouded by the pollination of rage throughout childhood. Only an ascending path remains and HE forgives all.

Immoral Invisibility

Wisdom and knowledge are needed to understand the words written by our ancestors. Applying the message of kindness and love is only mired by the unseen power of evil. Overcome the darkness that looms by rebuking with conviction in Faith.

Pardon

Forgiveness to cruel acts committed in the past must come from deep within the heart in order to truly commence a new beginning. Analyze the objective behind what punishment is required to reach satisfaction. Judge your actions in the evaluation of the verdict you would like to issue.

Sacramental Lamb

Innocently asking the LORD to transfer the excruciating pain of a loved one's migraine would be mimicked even today. The boundaries to what will be surpassed in the prevention of suffering will be difficult to establish. Compassion for those who lack the strength of self-preservation is the reasoning behind His sacrifice.

Peace

The environment created by the attitude portrayed is the reaction received whenever the personal boundary is invaded. Developing character traits will improve those who may be attracted or their approach will definitely be altered. When tranquility moves in there is no room for the strains of life.

Blame

When the spinning wheel of life has landed on a black hole, surrounding bodies tend to release their gravitational pull. Input comes from several resources but the output has only one undisputed supplier. Be careful not to point the finger in a room full of mirrors.

No Surrender

The path of life may become obstructed and take you to the edge of existence, but Faith is the transfer ticket which grants an extension. Though the road that is traveled has always been painted as thorny, one must be reminded that the bearer of the crown is in control of the strokes. Giving up is not an option when you think of the innocent dependents.

Consequences

Admire the Grace in the stillness of the water. Do not be tempted to stir up the mud which lies dormant, the chaos causes a distorted vision of the contents and the possibility of stepping onto the spines of a blameless urchin. Repercussions of malice have a greater impact at the unprotected journey's end.

Repercussion Default

Forgiven for the trespasses of the past ought to attain the peace that is promised with the act. Reneging on the deed will bring a multitude of consequences from the highest of authorities. I will keep you in my prayers.

Prayer

Reprimand the unclean essence that continuously attempts to deprive the joy which has been bestowed upon you. Announce with vigor the strength of the shield that protects with the gift of Grace. Palms up and head bowed as the request is submitted with humility and love.

Foolish Reign

The advantage will be in your favor for a limited time when treating the gullible with disrespect. Innocence is heavily guarded by winged spirits who have no problem executing the vengeance warranted by the acts of imprudence. Ugly behavior is frowned upon and is usually very costly.

Mass Destruction

Avoid the risk of damaging an object if a replacement is not on hand. Souls are items that are a single issue, so do not make it easy for it to fall into the wrong hands. Once the transaction is complete, you will waste an eternity with ill attempts to recover on your own. Contrary to popular belief, Prayer is the most powerful weapon known to man.

Final Judgment

The panel of judges consists of one so the campaign must be from the heart as anything else will fall on deaf ears. Fear is realizing that the jury is made up of one of the judges on the panel. A deliberation which takes long is due to the coin landing on its side.

Rewards of the Explored

Set aside one day of the month to enjoy a vacation, one day a week for yourself and every day to give thanks to GOD for its existence. Explore the unknown which surrounds you. Pamper yourself whenever possible. Pray with conviction and witness His Grace.

A Blessed Gift

Many years of being the consoler, the educator, the disciplinarian, the source of income, and the pillar of Love, has been an investment with bountiful returns. A family that continues to spread the roots of our ancestors aspires of becoming part of the Almighty's flock. Thank you, Heavenly Father, for the nurturing you continue to provide.

The Love App

Feeling the fear of the unknown as you watch your crops cultivate may be a fertilizer for anxiety. Remain faithful that the tools will be provided when the need becomes apparent. Enrichment during the development of the product will come directly from the proportion of Love that is applied.

Acquittal

Accusations compare to a cold front which usually brings in the drop, in temperature. Reassuring yourself that will soon change is the inspiration needed to get through those uneasy times. Trust in Him to expose your innocence and it shall be granted while clearing your name.

No Color Additives

Lean forward with trust in the invisible safety net. Though unseen by the naked eye, the grip of each citizen with their fellow neighbor in times of crisis is the cross stitch that has mended our differences. GOD's blessings do not have their precedence set in colors by numbers but granted by the love for one another.

Transparency

When bail is paid, there will still be a chance of being found guilty including luxury room and board in the local correctional facility. Be sure to clear the slate by asking for forgiveness. Remember that there is only one judge and He has the capability of looking into your heart.

Masterpiece, GOD Sent

Resentment sets in for many reasons as the load gets heavier. The body transforms into an unattractive storage facility with precious cargo in its cocoon. When the delivery arrives the magnitude of GOD's awe is a visual that lasts a lifetime.

Creator's Awe

Though the venue changed along with the significant other, the result remained as natural as the Lord blessed it. The equipment used to monitor the process showed the advancement of technology but the labor and delivery shows that perfection should be left alone. An undefined marvel bestowed by the Creator.

New Beginnings

Be proud to be envied. There is no secret in giving without prejudice the return is so powerful that it illuminates the darkness. Use the energy to believe and the path out of the shadows will glow with smiles of your transformation.

Obligation without Intent

Generosity can be a form of therapy though there may be many unfortunate imposters. A true giving heart can feel the dishonest vibration and choose to divert funds. Do not give in to the thoughts of what will be done with the gift.

Episode III

Effort

The Flow of Life

The pursuit of happiness is a long journey. Only you know the value of the souvenirs that were collected along the way. A wave will not hit the shore twice, but no worries, another will follow...

Tenacity

Never underestimate the will from within. Life's lessons appear right before our eyes, yet we choose not to see them. The strong current and the powerful slashing of a bear's claw do not deter the mission of the salmon...... Are you there????

Forte

It may be beneficial to your heart to rehearse your maneuvering skills in the event of a potential head on. There are many ways to be cable-towed. Be advised, it is not the power of the lead vehicle but the strength of the rope that is in question.

Gossip

A Wise man once said that at the birth of a bitch, her ass is removed and attached to another bitch, so they spend the rest of their life sniffing each other's ass in search of their own.... Is that a wig?

Watch Your Step

An act of desperation will alarm the enemies of an approach. Reanalyze the three steps before and the clue of plan malfunction may become evident. Construe the writing on the wall as assistance to avoid your demise. Is the manure smell coming from your leather personnel carriers?

Zip It

Though it may seem outlandish to grow patience in rocky terrain, there should be more effort applied in nurturing and cultivating so that fruit may be produced. At times the right amount of torque will keep the tongue from lashing out idiotically.

Invisible Profit

A generous dose of giving will be rewarded with an unforeseeable amount in return. Add a pinch of positivity to all your recipes for a more flavorsome result. Baking soda and water, stirred not shaken, will unravel the knots of negativity.

Total Disregard

Repetitions of reasons, which cause irritability, were difficult enough the first time they were mentioned. Totally ignoring issues will not evaporate them from sight. Want to listen instead of listening to what you want.

The Value of Education

The manner, in which a lesson is taught, is judged on how perfect it is repeated. Force fed dictatorship, may lead to rebellious behavior and all out mutiny. Breaking the seal of a closed mind will energize the light bulb.

Obstacles

Caution is advised when driving by a cliff, as unexpected falling boulders may hinder or veer you from your path. Bugs are fine in the weeds, it is when the attempt to cross a crowded path that they are subject to being squashed. Concrete has no power over the tenacity of a tree root.

Chemistry

Patience is self-taught and involves many compounds in the formula. Personalities may gel at the start but if the equation is done at haste there may a negative reaction. Acceptance of nature taking its course exhibits nobility.

Shared World

Freedom to roam wherever you want may suddenly be restricted. Though the intentions are not of malice the results can be terminal. When roaming is done together without boundaries, what has been observed is much more beautiful.

Fine Tuning

Lack of ability to social interact should not be a hindrance to the construction of confidence. Chemistry can be difficult to comprehend but it is the difference that makes us unique. Don't exhaust your effort attempting to be like someone else when perfecting who you are should be the concentration of your studies.

Determined Success

In the attempt to avoid economic hardship, raw talent may be hidden by the need to settle for a low number on the "desired opportunity" list. Make your dreams reality by a persistent drive on the road to self-achievement. If a brilliant thought crosses your mind then act on it, the reward may be an unexpected treasure.

Sweet Revenge

Intimidating the obviously uneven matched will find its way back with a vengeance. The physical advantage produces thoughts of superiority, but beware that retaliation is being carefully planned. You seemed so much bigger when I was a kid!

Unpractical Joke

Removing the splinter with the fire sanitized safety pin was with good intention. The evil act was not heating up the wrong end, but causing it to blister the uninjured hand. What may seem funny should be completely thought out because the guilty memory will stay with you forever.

Defy Without Glory

Worn out gym shoes, a red Clemente signed baseball glove, and dreams of becoming a professional ball player was all that was needed to outperform the large group of twelve-year old's. The boundary limitations were not adhered to and the punishment for the violation was not an obstacle yet to be overcome.

Hidden Knowledge

Due to the pressures of poverty, childhood memories were of chores beyond the capabilities of an unmotivated adolescent. Though there were a variety of skills developed they were only understood after the need was demanded. Take advantage of whatever the lesson is presented to you, its value will be unmasked in due time.

Foul Contents

Dragging feet to have an advantage over a situation may unevenly wear out shoes and cause a limp when walking. Results from conniving acts, lead to a life of misery. Removing the wrinkles may disguise the outer appearance but exposed lies uncover the ugliness that always resided.

Integrity

A community workspace may lead to false accusations. Stand firm with the truth that resides in a clear conscience. When the cargo is precious, a righteous man will insure that the straps are inspected constantly as to not lose the entire payload.

Apprehensive Hindrance

Sincerity is felt in the heart, but don't attempt to block an honest effort. Suspicious thoughts for all that surrounds you are a true indication that the conquering of inner peace still is a work in progress. Allow the self-modification process to complete the upload of the input analysis software.

Upgraded Performance

An allocation of time allows a frustrated fool to seek self-improvement and realize how inappropriate his behavior has been interpreted. Humbleness accompanied with a request for forgiveness will soften any anti-idiot barrier. Evaluators give credit to self-observed infractions with corrective actions attached.

Wary Wall

Blinded by the need to defend a point of view may cause hearing loss. Out of body experience should be done immediately to see past the glare of arrogance. The wrinkles in the disagreement of terms can truly be ironed out with forgiveness and love.

Confidence Construction

Quit the continual critical self-evaluation by applying the one step at a time of smoothing out rough edges. Repetition of corrected behavior develops into sophisticated mannerisms in the presence of loyalty. The change of your reflection will only depend on the effort applied.

Mentor

Impressions of a madman are so easy to remember if the actions are witnessed by a vulnerable victim. Make an attempt to guide those souls that are exposed to unscrupulous behavior to improve their opinion of Grace. Lead by the example that caused the right choice at the fork in the road.

Message Quality

Opportunities to share your knowledge should not give off a sense of burden. The pupil will sense if the wisdom that is being received has been dipped in sarcasm. Sincerity in your tone will determine the quality of the comfort zone and the development of a mind.

Attention to Detail

I applaud those who can retain all they read. The contents may come as a blend of very well versed scholar losing grip with common sense. Listen to what is being broadcasted as if you were the one holding the microphone.

Backyard Lawyer

It is far less complicated to guess and hope to get it right than to research the true facts. If your predictions have been right lately you should quit while you are ahead. Accusations have caused the innocent a lot of headaches.

Sincere Pleasantry

Friendliness has hidden benefits that surface when the recipient's heart is touched. Though the outer cover looks complicated it does not mean it is impenetrable. Ugliness is not due to appearance but to the manner in which the heart presents it.

Aggressive Politeness

Impressions left behind should leave the taste of a fine wine instead of a sour apple. Those that provide service may have a bad day on the same day that you are at your worst. Deep digging is required to be the better person and it may be contagious.

Self Service

Leave an impression on those who have extended their humble abode as billets for the duration. Actually, treating the facilities above and beyond should surpass the expectations of your own dwelling. The management may cut the stay short for untidy behavior.

Reward Fine Print

Gratitude is valued by the way it is shown not by eloquent words that carry no weight. An offer to return with an open date is proof that behavior during the visit was acceptable. Instill those same standards when the offspring are accompanying baggage.

Watering Hole

Utilizing your residence as a reception station prior to a move to permanent quarters can be a costly experience. Role of the only meeting place for gatherings will give an impression of not wanting to visit others in the inner circle. Mandatory visits only apply to those without the capability of transportation or with bed ridden illnesses.

Unfaithful Resources

Greed will temporarily fulfill a desire to live better than others but in the long run the world will become a very lonesome place. Funds that were earned by one that has placed country before self should not be shared with infidelity. Caution, a two-way mirror is being used to watch every move.

Respect Instructor

The pocketbook holds the identification of the owner and is considered personal property. Without consent or authorization foreign fingers should abide by the privacy policy to ensure an extended shelf life. Good home training awards are seldom having the honor of being hung on the good character wall due to the lack of descent cadre.

Other's Agony

Pain so intense it opens the eye secretion valves regardless of the audience. Ice directly applied reduces the inflammation without including the pride and the brace restricts any ill-advised movement. Sympathy can at times be interpreted as the relief of not being the bearer of the pain.

Closed for Sound

Arrogance should not be an ingredient which is added to an opening statement because it may have a sign flipping reaction. Excessive volume increase will cause protective covers to secure the inner drums. Alarms must clear for the obstacles to be removed.

Twin Metamorphosis

Though the outer image was made to be similar, there are very unique signs of tampering. If a dissection of a monster's mind is conducted there will be evidence of the seal being broken. Seek guidance if the instructions become too difficult to follow.

Angel Tears

Without a sound the formation is made and the free-fall ends on the transparent surface. Soon others find the exact spot and once there is enough gravity perform its duty and the journey begins. Though it may be a short phase to roll down the eye which follows enjoys the serenity of a rain drop's existence.

Vows

If you must remember when things were good, it only expresses that the effort has diminished. The investigation should be of the turning point not of the blame. The desire to continue must be mutual so that all wheels roll in the same direction.

Egotistic Obligation

Greed from those in your group may leave just a few crumbs to be shared by the end of the line. The lack of leadership shows that "self", alphabetically trumps "subordinate". The guide's responsibility should not include paper weight as top priority.

Humbleness

Outside the castle the kingdom is becoming chaotic but be advised that the inner guards will shoot then ask what are the intentions. Remove the battle gear before approaching the King or the approach will be interpreted as an act of aggression. War heroes still must answer to a higher authority.

Episode IV

Egotism

The Last Drop

Black gold is a rare commodity with an Alpha and an Omega. Enjoy my glamorous views on the slow beautiful trip to the tip of my mountain. For the return is much faster and steep with no opportunity to savor my scenery. The sudden impact will be into my grey womb smothered in chaos. Wake up, you're killin' me.

Inflamed Smoke

Chest poked out with the responsibility of being the man of the house may lead to a swollen head and Napoleon-like symptoms. The act of being over shielding to someone may be interpreted by them as being the victim rather than the protected. Humbleness will always prevail over the power of the brawn.

Button Pushed

The swelling will be affected only if the ice is held in place. The puffiness around the eyes was not a result of a lack of sleep. Provoking the deliverance can be avoided when the threshold that is known is surpassed.

Demeaning Revolt

The power to change is limited to the image in the mirror. Forcing your policies on the rebellious only ignites the individualism residing in that opposing party. Tread carefully as mutiny is brewing within the crew. Talking down will cause an uprising.

A Snap Away

Testosterone levels collide when the first born becomes aware of their strength. The constant bumps to the head rearrange the priorities of what career field will be followed. The huge heart is clouded by the rage that was fertilized throughout childhood. Steel thread has started to fray.

When in Rome

Culture shock is one of the preliminary stages to develop a world traveler. Foreign land and language are challenges that are soon overcome by the warmth of the natives. The respect received is much greater with a valid attempt to acculturate.

Walgreen's Wonder

Winner of the contest, please claim you prize. A title may be a play on words for marketing purposes yet can cause a terrible embarrassment. Boat and Snow should be a deadly giveaway to a dead giveaway. Don't boast as the Jones until you have a visual.

Foreign Feel

Physical contact will lead to an unusual reaction from even the mildness of men. Remove your hand on your own accord or enjoy the bouquets at funeral home. Weather calls for a slight shower of hard knocks and hail as natural ice packs.

Exhausted Opportunities

Luggage made of hefty is carefully placed away from the trash. Relocation of attitude is awarded a first-class ticket to anywhere but here. Tolerance is low for the lack of intelligence. Be wise to abort the thought of confrontation when the house bets against you.

Flat Zeal

Talent may give the edge on the popularity chart yet it is not enough for the egocentric individual. Picking on the meek does not give the crown anymore luster than it has, in fact dullness begins to set in. Humbleness is the ingredient which gives shine its brilliance.

Trigger Happy

A shield is used to protect and overwhelm an opponent but in the wrong hands the level of authority may inflate the ego. Right to bear arms has left some without dignity. Only five pounds of pressure may decrease freedom by five to ten years.

Exposed Development

Time and the belief of a higher power ripen the aging youth. Maturity is not an ingredient that is found on a shelf but a seed that is nurtured by those who create. Pleasure and pride comes when the product is visually reaped.

Gluttony

An overindulgence of anything will become evident upon capacity's limit. Regardless of the size of the appetite an inner alarm sounds when the danger zone has been reached. It becomes painfully obvious when the symptoms of greed have conquered sound judgment.

Vain in the Vein

Turning the spotlight towards yourself may not only blind you but shed light on the shortage of intelligence. The trip on the last step will definitely be more of an impact than the reason you appeared on the stage. Blushing tones are not at all complementary.

Discharging Rage

Short fuse on an explosive device can make it sensitive and cause an early release of fury. It may behoove you to invest in purchasing a longer ignition cord to allow time to prevent the explosion. Pressure release button should be pressed regularly.

Premature Disruption

Victory may come in the manner in which defeat is handled. Though the opportunity has not yet been granted to implement an alternate ideology, one must support the current policies. Criticisms of a plan half way completed can be viewed as not only an interruption but as an inability to play well with others.

Instruction-less

If the plans are followed correctly there may be a significant amount of pride in the construction of a dog house. Your ability to stay out of it upon its completion will be greatly appreciated by the primary resident. "Yes dear", are key words to real comfort.

Detail Reward

It is not the weight of what is above the last man on the totem pole that he should be concerned with but the waste that trickles down. Until a new hire comes on board, a "newbie" will be awarded all the unpopular duties. Be attentive and proud as knowledge can be disguised in the simplest manner.

Disco Ball

Anticipation grows high as the time approaches to meet the princess. In hopes of making an impact the mind races with thoughts for the right monologue. The root cause of happiness does not lay in the acceptance of neither but in the acknowledgement of the Queen's happy ending.

Character Curtain

A rubber mask can change the personality of the wearer and also protect the exposure of ugly. It is an opportunity to act like a fool unless your occupation is being a clown. Be sure to adjust to reality but realize how much pleasure you acquired from the conversation.

Vertical Stretch

The meaning of "Love thy neighbor" has changed dramatically as technology has replaced the face to face interaction with a cyber-society. Saying hello the moment eye to eye contact has been rehearsed to a photo in an effort to achieve perfection. Caution as altering software can cause regurgitation.

The Dirty I

When the reflection witnesses the foul act, it becomes inerasably etched in memory. No matter the change in color of the hair or the style of the attire, the integrity will continue to be scarred. The visual transparency of the uncouth deed will be inescapably present when the silhouette collides with the mirror.

No Guarantee

It boggles the mind to think that a catastrophic uncommon climate change does not convince the skeptical until they are neck deep in contaminated water. There are small indications that the abuse to our natural resources will not be tolerated any longer. Dooms day "preppers" after exhausting the little life left will be surprised if their names are not on the list.

Alternate Approach

A work around should be considered to avoid connection loss. Either the issue falls on the lack of redundancy or just engineering ignorance. A misinterpreted message can be redirected for improved clarity. Self-appointed attention can make it easy to find a scapegoat to reprimand.

Confidence Overdraft

It is clear that one of the reasons for allies is to keep bullies from taking things by force. The relationship needs to be verified before poking out your chest against a heavy weight. Imaginary funds cannot pay for the physical harm received when the check bounces.

A Good Weave

Consistency in your history results in a pretty accurate prediction of your actions. Make an attempt to correct your imperfections in order to allow the injuries to heal. A slight movement to the left can prevent outpatient surgery.

Work in Progress

Due to the frustration felt in a body malfunction, there should not be aggressive action towards a garbled message. The bark of a poodle, though very annoying, cannot start to receive the fear of a Sheppard. There are still some kinks that have to be worked out in the new model so approach cautiously.

Move On

Control insecurities before the infiltration causes the exploitation of rational thinking. From this point on the process for the heart to be conquered only includes you. It is ludicrous to be inserted into someone else's past.

Inner Splendor

Make-up artist have not been able to cover up the ugliness of the heart. When the lights of the vanity come to the end of their lives beauty should be seen even by a blind man. The construction of a new beginning starts from within.

Confidentially Speaking

A starting point changes coordinates according to the individual. Negative critiques will only throw off their azimuth and vacuum the wind out of their sail. Even a Boxer cheers for himself before his back is on the canvas accompanied by a circle of birds.

Episode V

Surmise

The Virtue of Patience

Disappointment is a direct result of expectation. The anticipation of an occurrence may leave you in suspense forever. Prospects may lower the standard, but hope will increase the Return On Investment.

On Your Mark

Expectations may lead to disappointments, but there must be a starting point. There is no sense for the competition if the participants fail to show up. You will forfeit for not appearing, though the competitor has conceded.

Pains of Growth

The disappointment of not meeting an expectation can only be as heavy as the pity that you feel for yourself. Every experience is a potential for personal evolution. Damn.....better fasten that back brace, this S H and I T weigh a ton.

Hurry Up and Wait

Temporary medication should be prescribed for prolonged standing in a pharmacy line. Procedures to distribute cures need to be diagnosed as well. No use to call in the order the day before, when data entry is performed after a forty-minute wait to reach the window. "Now have a seat, your name will appear on the monitor in an hour or so" …

Required Duty

Though the form may be official, the request may be ridiculous. The position's title should be researched before tasks are misrouted. Never spit straight up, what returns just isn't the same.

Worth the Wait

Unless you have met the person on the image, judgment should not be concluded from a two-dimensional portrait. It is the third dimension which gives life to a photograph. Though the frame may be aged the contents within its border is what holds the value.

Smooching Not Allowed

At times, no matter how well you pack an item, you still end up with damaged goods. Greasing the wheels will enhance the length of a free ride. Precedence on priorities will become a reality, now that they are your own.

The Square Diamond

Protective gear has been invented to give confidence on unexpected bounces. Forgetting to insert it into the specially made pocket may change the octet level of your voice. The choice has been made easy to change your career path as the memory still makes you wince.

Green Monster

Volcanoes are a thing of beauty when in a dormant state but when the inner core is aggravated the eruption is unconceivable. Mild manners should not be mistaken as a pin cushion for the aggressive as an explosion with the force of a category five may remove a limb. Surprises will ensue the pushing of the wrong button.

A to the Z

A dare carried out may become more expensive than the purse being awarded. At times, what was done for a laugh turns out to be an exhausting flow of tears or perhaps a void in the front grill. Could you find the humor of the tables turning?

Ejected

Being a fan is not equivalent to being a gang member. The colors worn are part of being a fanatic of a favorite team not a threat to another's way of life. Be advised that the title of adult comes with a strict obligation of growing up!

Instilled Faith

It is not worth an aneurism to stress over what has happened unless the powers of reverse are in your control. Impressive is the act of recovery when the odds have temporarily overcome you. The achievements accomplished deserve the gratitude due to those who believed from the start.

Irretrievable Matter

The technology which has catapulted us into the future must be handled with caution when the eyes are to be concentrated on what is on the other side of the windshield. A split second to glimpse at the screen may cause an operator dome split or the irreversible manslaughter charge.

Limits

Do not stress what has not found the right track. Understand that there is always a second opinion that contradicts a great idea. Approach cautiously the delivery angle so that the bend does not break.

Preferences to Engage

There is comfort of residing within a community where the majority is composed of a certain ethnic group. In the past, this action was considered segregation but now it totally depends on the side of the law is concerned, the defense or the prosecution. Predicaments are constituted by choices.

The Imperial Guard

Paranoia of espionage due to the many years exposed to the "need to know" information can develop neck and shoulder issues. Eyes on the door and continual scanning of the surroundings allude to a high level of readiness. Wound too tight will shorten the friends list.

Example One

Panicked reaction causes the rational circuits to lose signal. Focus on options that will dispense positivity and realize sanity self-control is being monitored. Practice patience before it is required so what is provided is leadership.

Tactful Tongue

Devious responses due to the improper analysis of the lesson may cause impressions of disrespect. The respect due to the rank goes without saying yet a remark strategically placed will gain a higher return. The mind twisting question sometimes receives an answer far from what was expected leaving the interrogator speechless.

Check Yourself

The cracking sound is similar to what is heard when stepping on thin ice but actually it is the egg shells left behind from the atmosphere adjustment. Realize that humbleness has a breaking point when under new construction. Aggression may be painful when, the unexpected brick wall becomes the reason for the sudden halt.

Kid Brutality

The beautiful glowing red coil turned into a painful experience when there was an attempt to grab it. As the screams of pain took seconds to escape the shocked victim, those around the area lost their minds as they scrambled to recall their first aid procedures. Avoiding the rehearsal may cause a terrible performance and horrible memory.

Business as Usual

Hiring all engineers will cause a conflict in decision making. Expecting employees to be engineers will cause a leadership conflict. Ensure that those appointed as management have experienced the trenches or suffer the consequences of growing pains.

Conquering Odor

The reaction of personal space invasion can only be worsened by the intruder's halitosis range of destruction. Watering eyes during a non-sorrow conversation are evidence that mouth maintenance is required. It is not proper to share the aroma of food after it has been chewed and swallowed.

Unpleasant Garden of Eden

Adjustment to a culture while visiting another country can be a very foul experience when compared to the pleasant fragrances the senses are accustomed to. A method of attraction that involves total disregard to deodorant will definitely empty out a crowded room. Vagrant's maybe entitled to harems with bushy arm pits.

Rebirth

Accept the change before your eyes and the gifts that are attached. A sarcastic remark may cause flaws in items of convenience at the moment they are needed. Do not confuse humbleness that is shown on the next encounter as a meaning of victory for the receiver. Witness the definition of Man in true form by the host.

The Protruding Beam

The desire to find fault in another must be done with all fingers pointed towards the accused. Any reasonable doubt can be used to prove how personal it really is. If it needs to be secured, then secure it before the kindergarten mentality takes control and the clown makeup is applied. Say cheese for the hidden camera.

Masterpiece

Though the preference maybe different the intelligence level must be esteemed. Respect should always flow in both directions without reversing discrimination. It is not my judgment of how straight the grading curve should be where the concern should lie. He was not confused during his creation.

Pillar of Salt

A line must be drawn to divide the personal from the private without forgetting that even thoughts are heard by He who counts. Before the thought becomes an action take note of being the recipient. Generations are losing their innocence with the openness of fashion and minds.

Jealous Madness

Coupons should have their own lane to bottleneck. Not all have the patience of a collector or Bargain Betty, so instead of aggravation seek service from another cashier. It is not worth rupturing an artery over simple solutions to others ingenuities.

Episode VI

Astute

Learn to Teach

Wisdom is a direct result of inaccurate decision making. An oversight will adjust the focus of the intention. Be fearless of an opportunity to learn, because there will be followers that will need guidance not to recreate the error.

Joint Command

Generals are awarded credit for the war, though the victory is a direct result of battles won by the troops. Planning an attack on paper without consulting with ground commandos, will lead to the loss of life in the trenches. Though the skin is tough the mind will still shows signs of battle fatigue.

Human Hardware

Life has its phases, good or bad, however it is the intelligence of the operator who enables the equipment to perform its task. Settlement for contentment will fog the path to higher achievements. A step back may clear your vision to the success ahead.

Strict Guidelines

Giving a visual by drawing with crayon is not to question the intelligence of the audience but to ensure the speaker is coloring within the lines. The phrase "repeating exercise" provides evidence that the initial comment will be distorted by the end of the communication line. Failure to follow instructions may result in a spare parts list.

Ignorance Blossomed

Past experiences teach lessons to both ends of the spectrum. Parameters that are inputted into the equation change and as a result, the outcome changes as well. Use experiences as countermeasures to the negative results to neutralize the equation.

A Battle Choice

The cost of an itinerary change may be more than a tighter grip of the word formulator. The witty response may involve an extensive cab ride beyond the means of the budget. Though a long walk may clear your mind, it may tease the jagged teeth of frostbite.

Smell the Roses

Knowledge is only attained through the persistent research of information and is a direct result of the unraveling of a hypothesis. In the pursuit of the intellect what seemed to be extremely complex is fitted together like a grade school puzzle. The complexity is in the mind of the ignorant...scratch and sniff...

Sharp Sensors

Logical thinking may need to be used with different approaches when in the sites of a trouble shooter. The scent of a scoundrel is detected easily by the early warning system of a Taurus. Rethink your plan…it's in plain view. Only you are blind to the outcome.

Well Foundation

To attain knowledge from a veteran craftsman, turn slowly to the lefty for a steady flow of data. A firm twist to the righty is a preventive measure for information leakage. Pay attention and take notes because I will NOT be here all day.

Contaminated Emissions

Allergic reaction to the citrus in the drink may not be from the secretions of the acidic pulp but from the unclean outer coverings. The smell will usually give the indication of overdue sanitation practices. Wash the fruit before you eat it.

Consequences of Curiosity

The ice has not quite frozen over yet, but your curiosity does not keep you from walking on it. Take heed to the cracking sound. Though it is very shallow, a two-foot swallow of water can still cause you to drown.

Capacity Overload

Those riding the short bus and wearing the helmets form one line... OK, gather here... I will speak slowly and use crayons to enhance visual aids. Rudolph and Bambi, how many times have I told you not to look directly into lights...?

Endangered Resource

Sustainability calls for intelligence on the user's part. Replenish that which has been expended; there will be hard days ahead and preparation is required. Commodities change as well as face value. What today is a grape, tomorrow will become a raisin.

Hidden Means

Cope with the twist and turns that life presents. The ones that depend on you count on your best attempts. When a pit appears inescapable use the contents to build steps of resolve. Round edges will cause a slippery slope.

Liquid Courage

Consumption beyond limits has a way of building confidence and dissipating the capacity of intelligence. The police horse would fall over, not by power of the punch but from the laughter of the mere thought of it. Dressed like a superhero does not mean the special powers were included in the price of the costume.

Uncured Establishment

Building the level of experience comes from ensuring that every piece is in its proper place. A weak foundation is never evident until the top floor is complete. Instead of continuing the construction, all efforts are on the repair of incompetence.

Facade for Fear

Removing the base tie down pegs causes the ankle to snap. The look of fear in their eyes was what I needed to kill the pain. Morphine injection magically removes what was held in and instills a smile. Tolerance levels are controllable only if the desire is to disillusion the audience.

Box of Teeth

Ivory rectangles strategically numbered, challenge the wit of man. Objective is to rid the seven from your grips before the opponent has his chance. Forming a circuit by connecting both ends with one piece will initiate the verbal outburst of the word "Capicu"!

Taming the Wild

Intensity in your performance at times may not be noticed by an unobservant self-appointed slave master. The knowledge attained throughout the period of overwhelming stress is therefore the property of the beholder and can never be repossessed. The gift of information is what gives the strategic upper hand and produces the awareness of the advantageous predicament.

Pottery Bust

The change of elevation causes the loss of footing and the momentum rolls the body under the bush. The sound of thud whisks by at an incredible speed. After several moments of absolute stillness, the sound of asthma wheezing gives away the perfect hiding place. Forgetting to take medication may cause an imbalance in your existence.

Absorbed Academics

If by stating what goals will be achieved could actually become true in a blink of an eye, then the world would be filled with bored intellects. Act on the thoughts of improving that cross your mind or you will find tomorrow to be another day behind. The brain is a sponge with unlimited capacity, lay in every puddle of knowledge you may encounter.

The Riddle of Genius

Knowledge is attained by piecing together the puzzle of life. Patience is the tool which will grant the emotional gratification upon the completion of the task. Pursuing with haste will cause a flaw in the masterpiece and its value to be worthless.

Terms of Development

Encyclopedias retained volumes of knowledge that were forced to be opened. Time gave way to the reasons behind the pointing towards the bookcase. Advanced vocabulary was ridiculed as trying to be proper. Praise and honor were granted when the battle of wit was overwhelmingly in your favor.

Human OS

Upgrading the memory of a human is performed by repetition. Overload is reached when the limitation of capacity is surpassed. Fight pressure with an unruffled mentality, the mind will perform each task one command line at a time no matter the speed of the input.

Perseverance

No matter the amount of dislike felt for a job, one must not overlook the knowledge attained during the experience. Even the exposure to the ignorance of those in the surrounding environment will be a valuable lesson learned. Observation is the best collector of intelligence.

Good vs Evil

The functions of the human mind are inconceivable. With infinite calculations occurring, one thought will always have a minimum of two options. Though there may be many ways to take advantage of those around you, consider the consequences of the wrong choice.

Pass the Baton

Relinquish the grip on the wisdom acquired throughout the journey to develop those whose attention has been bitten. The seed will not grow without the nurturing of the caregiver. Encourage them to drink upon the arrival at the pond.

Visual Aides

A grant to extend a deadline is an opportunity to complete a thought and explain the solution of a complicated equation. A presentation in crayon will express the vision and allow room for creative criticism. Even a drawing of stick figures holding hands implies unity.

Opened Minded

Being volunteered for different tasks no matter its severity opens opportunities to build a firm foundation. Position yourself for exposure to unexplored areas of responsibility. Basic knowledge of all aspects that lead to a well-rounded base is the key to becoming a subject matter expert. All edges must be plumbed and squared before next level begins its construction.

Crash or Cruise

Any trade is difficult for the ignorant until the knowledge is attained. Those above will throw you into the fire either to get rid of the lack of confidence on your part or to smooth out the scheduling. Absorb as much as possible so the flames can remain manageable.

True Curriculum

Frustration is an emotion that is taught at an early age and is a result of adult expectations. Though the duty changes hand throughout life a parent is still the primary instructor. The curriculum should emphasize on the lesson instead of the performance.

Delayed Exit

Though the construction is performed with attention to detail the constant usage will weaken the joints. As the threats seem to proliferate in strength the antidote dosage is increased. Some things must complete their shelf life while new technology is developing replacement parts to prolong the inevitable. Careful stepping down when name is called.

Dam Sifter

Confusing a helping hand with that of an easy prey may cause the sound of the door slamming on potential support. The need to plug an ear to maintain information may be necessary to prevent it from escaping. Intelligence is attained by the desire to remove the layers of ignorance one at a time.

Earning the Eyeglass

Overloading of information continually exhausts the mind but memory space is infinite. Rid the fear of the unknown by persistently pursuing any and all knowledge that is offered. Time and education are what contribute to the growth of knowledge. Experiencing life attains wisdom.

Fool's Gold

Knowledge does not have a ceiling so anyone can be dethroned from being King "know it all". The pocket protector is not a symbol of wisdom; learn how to close the writing utensil so the shirt will not be ruined. Three stripes have their own troubleshooting techniques; the rocker that was added must have given a sense of sitting on the porch of the old folk's home.

Worthless Words

Having the last word may give you the impression that you have overwhelmed the other half. Doubt of the argument being cut short should question the rebuttal victory. The sudden end to a disagreement shows how low the opponent will want to reach.

Half the Distance

Though not blameless of the outcome, time should have been used to self-educate. Following the selfish guidance of the ignorant is easily contagious. Reading out loud without listening does not establish expertise.

Lecture Etiquette

As information flows through the listening devices connected to the body's CPU, air is released to activate the yawning process. The eye witness account formulates an opinion of boredom or of disinterest. A periodic question will retain respect in both directions.

Printed in the United States
By Bookmasters